99 blessings

...

9 9

blessings

. . . .

BROTHER DAVID STEINDL-RAST

. . . .

IMAGE
NEW YORK

www.crownpublishing.com

IMAGE is a registered trademark,
and the "I" colophon is a trademark
of Random House, Inc.

Library of Congress Cataloging-in-Publication Data

Steindl-Rast, David.
99 blessings / David Steindl-Rast. — 1st ed.
    p. cm.
1. Prayers.   2. Benediction.   I. Title.   II. Title:
Ninety-nine blessings.
BL560.S75 2013
242'.8—dc23

                    2012031083

ISBN 978-0-385-34794-5
eISBN 978-0-385-3475-01

PRINTED IN THE UNITED STATES OF AMERICA

Book design by Jaclyn Reyes
Jacket design by Jessie Bright

10   9   8   7   6   5   4   3   2   1

First Edition

*This little book is dedicated to
all things, plants, animals,
humans, and angels
that made me blessed
and able to bless.*

blessings

an invitation to bless

Listening closely, we can hear how similar they sound, the words *blessing* and *blood*. Blessing, rightly understood, is the invisible bloodstream pulsating through the universe—alive and life-giving. "Just to live is holy," says the great Jewish sage Abraham Joshua Heschel. "Just to be is a blessing."

"Bless what there is, for being." Whatever it be, bless it because it exists; you need no other reason. With those words the poet W. H. Auden summarizes "the singular command" with which the universe confronts us humans. Each page of this book invites you in a different way to rise to this challenge and "bless what there is for being."

For three months or so, I wrote these blessings down—one each day—blessing whatever happened to come to my mind, from insects to the Internet, from friendship to fresh linen. I resisted the temptation to "improve" them later; they stand here as they flowed from my pen. You might open the book at random and let yourself be surprised, or you might read these blessings—maybe one a day—in the order in which they were written. You might want to check the index of keywords and pick the blessing you need at the moment. I wish for you that you become aware of how greatly you yourself are blessed *and* eager to pass your blessings on. Passing them on is what counts.

Blessings are life-giving only as long as we pass them on. The waters of the river Jordan can teach us much about blessing: Fresh and refreshing, they leap down from the Lebanon Mountains, fill the Sea of Galilee to the brim, and make its shores an image of Paradise. Gardens, vineyards, and orchards are heavy with fruit and produce, and the lake itself teems with fish. Then these waters flow on, the Jordan continues, ending in the Dead Sea. What a difference here: The shores are barren desert, and no fish can survive in the briny water. But isn't it the same water? Yes, is the answer, indeed, it is the same water of blessing. But where blessing flows in and passes on, everything comes alive; where it flows only in and stops, it stagnates.

This accounts for the pattern of each blessing in this little book, first expressing delight in a blessing received, following with a resolution to pass it on. And this pattern is repeated over and over.

Repetition is the way time mirrors the eternal Now. Repetition with slight differences never fails to thrill our sense of beauty—a theme with variations in music, even a row of weathered fence posts along a paddock. Maybe our memory of the first sound that ever struck our budding ears in infancy, our mother's heartbeat when we were still daydreaming in her womb, gave us this love for repetition. And maybe the first stirring, then, of what would later mature into awe accounts for the important role that repetition plays in incantations and blessings. Allow yourself to feel its magic power. Ninety-nine times you will find it repeated here; the hundredth time I give you only the pattern for you to fill in some blessing that you welcome and want to pass on. Once you discover the joy this pattern can trigger, you will want to repeat it not just a hundred but innumerable times.

May this patchwork quilt of blessings help to sharpen your taste for the gift of life in its innumerable facets. May you grow ever more blessed, ever more able to bless.

1

SOURCE OF ALL BLESSINGS,

you bless us with **wind**.
Gentle or fierce, warm and humid
or icy or hot and dry, may it
caress my skin and make it tingle,
refresh my spirit and make it wide
awake so that I might to pass
on lightheartedness to everyone
I meet.

2

SOURCE OF ALL BLESSINGS,

you bless us with b r e a t h.
In and out, in and out, ever
renewing us, ever anew making us
one with all who breathe the same
air, may this blessing overflow
into a shared gratefulness, so that
with one breath I may praise and
celebrate life.

3

SOURCE OF ALL BLESSINGS,

you bless us every moment with
countless **hidden things** on
which our well-being depends,
though we will never know them—
from the water veins hidden deep
in the earth to the bacteria that
help us digest our food. May I pass
on blessings unnoticed for the
well-being of all.

4

SOURCE OF ALL BLESSINGS,

you bless us with fleeting
encounters—moments when
our path crosses just once with that
of another, whether the man who
holds a door open with a smile,
the receptionist who offers us a
kind word, or the child skipping
past us in the park. May these
blessings find me awake, alert, and
ready to pass on their gratuitous
sparkle by a sparkle in my own eye.

5

SOURCE OF ALL BLESSINGS,

you bless us with d r e a m s —
dreams while we sleep and dreams
in our most wakeful moments.
May I be responsive to both forms
of dreams and pass these blessings
on by living a life that is faithful to
their guidance.

6

you bless us with c o l o r s —
the strong and the subtle ones,
cornflower blue and poppy gold,
dragonfly-wing iridescence and
lichen silver. May my eyes and
my heart receive these countless
blessings sensitively and pass on
my joy to brighten all that lacks
light and zest.

7

SOURCE OF ALL BLESSINGS,

you bless us with moments in
which nothing happens—
moments of staring into the slowly-
burning-down fire, moments
waiting in the checkout line or
the waiting room. May I not fail
to expand into that wide-open
expanse of emptiness and pass on
this blessing of a wideness more
powerful than all anxiety in the
world.

8

SOURCE OF ALL BLESSINGS,

you bless us with healing
hands—hands of mothers and
lovers, of doctors and nurses, and
our own hands that are more gifted
with healing power than we know.
May I be alert to this gift and use
this power today whenever my
hands touch other human beings,
the fur of animals, or the slender
stems of flowers.

9

SOURCE OF ALL BLESSINGS,

you bless us with **music**—with the marvel that rhythms of drums and clapping of hands, the singing of flutes and the humming of strings, can send soul and body a-dancing and give us a sense of belonging to one another, to the whole, and to the force of life. May the ears of my heart be attuned to the silent music of the universe and swing with it.

10

you bless us with air travel—
that amazing human invention that
connects continents like the flight
of migrating birds and carries us
safely and in comfort more swiftly
than wing beat. May I use this gift
responsibly and see to it that my
traveling will not do more harm
to our planet than it does good to
people.

11

you bless us with friendship—
life's supreme gift, rare, precious,
and fragile. May I show myself
worthy of my friends by being
faithful, patient, and affectionate
while I have time to do so, aware
that all things are passing, even
firm friendships.

12

SOURCE OF ALL BLESSINGS,

you bless us with change—
in the seasons of the year, from
snow to greening, flowering,
fruiting, and harvest, in the
seasons of life, from childhood to
youth, full ripeness, and saging.
All living things keep changing.
May I welcome change as a sacred
opportunity to grow and savor
in each unrepeatable moment's
fleetingness what *Is* beyond
change.

13

SOURCE OF ALL BLESSINGS,

you bless us with departures —
for they are a necessary part of our
journey, necessary for arriving.
May I be always ready to take
leave, always aware that every
arrival is a prelude to departure,
every birth a step toward dying,
and may I thus taste the blessing of
being fully present where I am.

14

SOURCE OF ALL BLESSINGS,

you bless us with kinship with
all living beings—with the
fly who sits on the armrest of
my chair, spreads its wings, and
warms itself in the spring sunshine;
with the dog who tilts his head
and watches me like a child; with
the palm trees enjoying the same
breeze that fans my own skin. May
I honor that kinship by the respect
I show to all my kin.

15

SOURCE OF ALL BLESSINGS,

you bless us with candlelight—
that most domesticated of all fires,
and yet the same fire into which
our forebears gazed, generation
after generation, sitting around a
glowing fire pit under the stars, as
we are now sitting around a festive
table. May I carry that blessing so
vividly in my heart that it shines
in my eyes and in the eyes of all
whose eyes meet mine.

16

SOURCE OF ALL BLESSINGS,

you bless us with **medicines** for body and mind—herbs that we find in the wild, herbs that we plant and tend, healing concoctions created through human ingenuity, and all that strengthens, soothes, balances, and heals the mind. May I always find just what I need to keep myself well so that all I think and say and do will serve to heal others.

17

SOURCE OF ALL BLESSINGS,

you bless us with early-spring
flowers—the brave ones that get
snowed on, time and again, and
shine with joy between dead leaves
as they carpet the forest floor on
a sunny day, yet bear up under
any kind of weather. May I learn
from them the courage that comes
with the territory, bloom where I
am planted, and, no matter what
happens, radiate joy.

18

SOURCE OF ALL BLESSINGS,

you bless us with humility—
that down-to-earth quality that
has nothing in common with
humiliation but makes us stand
tall and acknowledge both the
humus that feeds us and the stars
to which we aspire. May I learn to
practice and to honor in others this
sparkling humility, which is the
dignity that we, as human beings,
cannot afford to lose.

19

SOURCE OF ALL BLESSINGS,

you bless us with humor —
our marvelous ability to smile at
the incongruities of our existence.
May the fissures in the structures
we build never make me anxious
or glum, but rather attentive to the
light that shines through the cracks
and ever ready to humor others
through that contagious humor,
which alone makes us truly human.

20

SOURCE OF ALL BLESSINGS,

you bless us with kitchen
noises—with the sound of
chopping carrots, the rumbling
from washing pots and pans, the
clinking of silverware, the clang of
glass on glass, the whistling of the
teakettle, and all the homey rattle
and clatter produced by preparing
food and washing dishes. May I
drink deeply from the blessing of
being at home that rings in these
sounds and make all whom I meet
today feel a bit more at home
in the world.

21

SOURCE OF ALL BLESSINGS,
you bless us with skillful
labor. What would we do without
the skill of workers who laid the
tile floor on which we walk, who
know how to make our toilets
flush, who keep our power stations
running smoothly? May I never
forget how much we depend on
them and on so-called unskilled
labor, which we'd be never able to
do for ourselves. May this blessing
flow through me as grateful
respect.

22

SOURCE OF ALL BLESSINGS,
you bless us with gravity—that
all-pervasive attraction that holds
all things together and determines
every one of our own movements
no less than the motion of planets,
stars, and galaxies. May I learn to
move with grace of both body and
soul by relying on a force on which
we can count, though we can never
explain it, and which holds all of us
together.

23

SOURCE OF ALL BLESSINGS,

you bless us with fresh linen—
its bleached whiteness, its clean
smell, its cool, smooth feel when
I fold it. May it remind me of the
fields where the flax from which it
comes stood blue in bloom, of the
hands that wove it, of the sacred
garments of the blessed, so that
I will rejoice in its blessings of
nature and culture and mystery,
and pass them on by my joy.

24

SOURCE OF ALL BLESSINGS,

you bless us with all that
cannot be expressed in
words—the nameless threat that
makes us shudder in the midst of
delight, or the urge that drives our
deepest longing, the dream beyond
our dreams, and the awe that
takes our breath away. May I learn
from all that makes me speechless
both the limit of words and their
glory, so that I will use them with
reverence.

SOURCE OF ALL BLESSINGS,

you bless us with l a k e s —
those eyes of the countryside that
look up to heaven, those mirrors
of the sky's every mood. For
the ever new surprise of water's
edge—rock, reed, or brush with
all their hidden life—for fish and,
farther out, boats, for wide water
moved by the wind or still, may I
be always grateful, and may I share
Earth with all who share this home
of ours.

26

SOURCE OF ALL BLESSINGS,

you bless us with potted plants.
Undeterred by their complete
helplessness, they prove so helpful
to those on whom, in every
way, they depend, offering their
fragrance, their taste, their healing
power, and above all, their beauty.
May I learn to graciously accept
helplessness and dependence
in all its forms and to serve,
nevertheless, by doing and by
being.

27

SOURCE OF ALL BLESSINGS,

you bless us with **warning
voices**—poets, prophets,
thinkers who dare to speak against
the current of accepted norms, to
question, at the risk of their good
standing, their careers, even their
lives. May I have ears to hear these
lonely voices of Common Sense,
so often nearly drowned out by the
din of public opinion, and to heed
them, take their message to heart,
weigh it, and let it change my life.

28

SOURCE OF ALL BLESSINGS,

you bless us with t e a r s —tears
of sorrow and tears of joy, tears
of outrage and of overwhelming
beauty. May I let them flow freely,
especially the waters that rise up
when the ice of anger cracks and
thaws in my heart, and the flood
tides of an oceanic feeling deep in
my heart that wash my eyes from
within and make me gentle toward
others.

29

SOURCE OF ALL BLESSINGS,

you bless us with e v e n i n g —with the fading of daylight, the lighting of lamps, the sleepiness, the going to sleep, that grants to both pain and pleasure a limit. May I find comfort inside, when animals stay in the wide outdoors while we humans enter under a roof to be together or to be alone, and may I never forget the homeless who somewhere fall asleep, too.

30

SOURCE OF ALL BLESSINGS,

you bless us with sparrows—
everywhere in the world the same
gray-and-brown mottled, noisily
chirping, ever hungry feathered
beggars on pavements and under
the tables of sidewalk cafés,
fighting for crumbs. May I learn
from these small relatives who
welcome me in Paris, Chicago,
Hong Kong, Moscow, and Tokyo
to be at home wherever I am and to
make others feel at home.

31

SOURCE OF ALL BLESSINGS,

you bless us with m e m o r y—
that sacred ingathering of the past
into the present that allows us to
recognize faces, learn poems by
heart, find our way back when we
are lost, and bring forth old and
new from its nearly inexhaustible
store. May I know what to forgive
and forget and what to retain and
treasure, keeping in mind the
smallest kindness shown to me
and spreading its ripples for a
long time.

32

SOURCE OF ALL BLESSINGS,

you bless us with the Internet,
the mind web that spans the earth
and gives us access to a vast
treasure-house of information;
it connects us with friends and
allows us to work with people we
will never know. May I take up the
challenge of those who laid this
technical foundation and help build
on it an invisible temple for sharing
and healing.

33

SOURCE OF ALL BLESSINGS,

you bless us with old fences—
wind-beaten ones that have lost
many a rail, rotten ones between
moss-covered posts, pasture
fences now standing in woods that
grew up on both sides of them,
garden fences leaning more aslant
with every spring. May I age
as gracefully as these charming
reminders that sooner or later
nature unites again what we divide.

34

SOURCE OF ALL BLESSINGS,

you bless us with young
animals, for we recognize them
at a glance, not only calves and
signets but baby newts and baby
bees; not only still-blind kittens
and birth-wet foals but newly
hatched snakes and crocodiles
pluck at our heartstrings. May I
make this blessing of affectionate
recognition flow out to living
beings of any age in celebration of
an all-connecting motherliness.

35

SOURCE OF ALL BLESSINGS,

you bless us with s n o w —
the first flakes rustling on autumn
leaves, the steady sleepy snowfalls
of midwinter, the late, wet flakes
whirling around tulips in full
bloom; the dense curtain, the
fluffy cover on twig and ledge,
the white garment of peaks and
slopes in glorious sunshine. May
this multiform blessing inspire me
to find ever new ways to celebrate
life. Just as no two flakes are alike,
never are two gestures of kindness
the same.

36

SOURCE OF ALL BLESSINGS,

you bless us with insects—
a blessing we do not appreciate
when mosquitoes bite us, flies buzz
around the table, or ants get into
our food supplies; and yet . . .
May I never cease to marvel
at the eyes of bees, the wings
of butterflies, the legs of
grasshoppers; and may I have
deep respect for all these our older
siblings in the family of creatures
that enjoy this earth and, like us,
breathe its air.

37

SOURCE OF ALL BLESSINGS,

you bless us with spoons and
forks—not only do they help
us eat soup and keep our fingers
clean, but they connect us, above
all, in ways we rarely consider.
May I be aware of my communion
with my parents, grandparents, and
their parents when I use old family
silver, and, in restaurants, of my
communion with guests who had
the same utensils in their mouths
that I am taking in my mouth,
consciously celebrating that bond.

38

SOURCE OF ALL BLESSINGS,

you bless us with times and seasons—bringing in their course birthdays, saints' days, and holy days, ever recurring in their cycles, yet ever new when they arrive. May I be steadied by their rhythm, from the rising of sap to sprouting, blossoming, and fruiting, falling of fruit and leaves and of the first snow; may I give myself to the flow of this great circle dance that carries us and joins us together.

SOURCE OF ALL BLESSINGS,

you bless us with t e a —that gift
of earth, water, fire, and air for
our enjoyment and for the healing
of body and mind. May I ever
more attentively learn to know
and appreciate teas and their
properties, and celebrate, as I sip,
these gifts of earth, the gentleness
of water that carries them, the
power of fire that heats them,
the flow of air that wafts their
fragrance, and, above all, the joy
of conviviality in sharing them.

40

SOURCE OF ALL BLESSINGS,

you bless us with b r e a d —
"fruit of the earth and work of
human hands," gift of nature and
of culture, primary image of all
food, and symbol of our human
communion around a worldwide
table. May I eat each morsel of
bread with a gratitude that implies
outrage at hunger; may I grow ever
more famished for a justice that
distributes food fairly and do all I
can until every child on earth has
bread enough.

41

you bless us with **wine** that
gladdens human hearts—gladdens
but also enslaves them, has done so
for some eight thousand years or
more, and continues to do so today.
May I, with every clinking of
goblets and every sip I take, marvel
at the ancient art of making wine,
delight in the color, fragrance, and
taste of this noble drink, remember
with compassion alcoholics, and
learn right measure.

42

SOURCE OF ALL BLESSINGS,

you bless us with fruit trees—
apple trees, fig trees, peach trees
heavy with their bounty; branches
weighed down by mango, papaya,
and avocado; young trees, fenced
in and propped up, and old ones,
still bearing abundantly; and whole
orchards in endless white veils of
blossoms or rich with the fragrance
of ripe fruit. May I, like these
trees, let the generosity of earth
flow through me and share it in
self-forgetful giving.

43

SOURCE OF ALL BLESSINGS,

you bless us with constellations—
Orion, the Pleiades, the Big
Dipper, images that a hundred
generations of our ancestors have
seen in the night sky and that, as
children, we have learned to name,
although the stars in each one
have no more in common than any
haphazard combination of stars.
May they teach me courage to trust
in images that have power to create
order out of chaos, courage to use
that magic power.

46

SOURCE OF ALL BLESSINGS,

you bless us with the smell of
leather, earthy, evoking so wide
a range of memories—my mother's
kid-leather gloves, the lederhosen
of my childhood, new briefcases,
old baseball mitts, the backseat of
a sports car, a butcher's apron in
a slaughterhouse. May my sense
of aliveness stretch and stretch to
welcome and embrace that broad a
spectrum of life.

47

SOURCE OF ALL BLESSINGS,

you bless us with pipe-organ
music, with the sense of the
sacred it evokes in the Christian
tradition, be it played on a simple
tracker organ in a village church
or in a cathedral on an instrument
with ten thousand pipes. When
my heart is lifted by its lilting or
shaken by its thunder, may I never
miss the best part: the silence after
the last note.

48

SOURCE OF ALL BLESSINGS,

you bless us with Oriental
rugs—marvels of the
imagination, masterworks of
skillful fingers, though also mute
accusers of relentless toil. May I
walk on them as on holy ground in
reverence for the unknown laborers
who tied a thousand knots in every
stamp-sized area to conjure up
patterns of Paradise; and may the
beauty they created make me stand
up for the exploited.

49

you bless us with b i r t h d a y s —
once-a-year occasions to put those
whom we love center stage and tell
them, as best we can, how much we
love and admire them. May I never
miss these opportunities to express
to others my gratitude for what
they do and especially what they
are; may I celebrate each new day
as the world's birthday and treat
everyone as a birthday child.

50

you bless us with h a i r —all the
variations nature is playing on the
theme of hair: tassels on corncobs,
iris-blossom beards, velvet fuzz
on sage leaves, nettles' fiery
bristles, seaweed in waves, Indian-
summer gossamer threads, the fur
of bumblebees and beavers, foxes'
golden-fulvous tails, and our own
native attire of human hair. As I
delight in this wealth of forms,
may I sing praise.

51

SOURCE OF ALL BLESSINGS,

you bless us with old tunes —
melodies we learned on our
mothers' knees, hymns a thousand
years older than the churches
in which we now chant them;
dance tunes popular in our teens,
haunting snatches of classical
music, or merely the ditties of
radio commercials. May I sing
them and remember those who
sang them before me and those who
will sing them when I am gone.

52

SOURCE OF ALL BLESSINGS,

you bless us with courage—
yes, the rare outstanding courage
of rescue workers, martyrs,
mountaineers, and pioneers on the
forefront of thought and service,
but even more so the valor of
all who bear up under ordinary
hardship and the daily grind of
repetition, dead tired, yet with
a smile. May I remember their
unself-conscious gallantry and
imitate their brave kindness.

53

SOURCE OF ALL BLESSINGS,

you bless us with adornments—
the bracelets, rings, necklaces,
brooches, and earrings in today's
jewelry boxes or recovered from
millennia-old tombs; the golden
bangles of Egyptian princesses, the
bronze braces of a Viking warrior,
the bone beads from a Stone Age
grave. May these tokens exchanged
between long-ago friends keep me
aware of the beauty that springs
from fondness.

54

SOURCE OF ALL BLESSINGS,

you bless us with f o g —heavy
shrouds that dim the headlights
and make the traffic slow down,
white ghosts creeping across the
pastures before sunrise, plumes
that float up from valleys after
the rain, see-through veils of the
moon. May I see it for what it truly
is: not a metaphor for all that limits
our vision of ultimate reality but
that reality showing itself in one of
its countless expressions.

55

SOURCE OF ALL BLESSINGS,

you bless us with views from
train windows—landscape
that rotates one way near the
tracks and the opposite way near
the horizon, while we sit back and
watch it rolling by like a film,
yet real and with a life of its own.
May I always live keenly aware of
worlds unaware of being observed,
worlds turning and touching,
separate from each other, yet one.

56

SOURCE OF ALL BLESSINGS,

you bless us with archetypes —
king, jewel, dragon, labyrinth,
orphan, journey, blue flower, and
all the other images that play out
their stories in the life story of
each of us. May I find my role, my
roles, in this age-old play on the
stage of the world and play them
well, taking them both seriously
and lightly, never forgetting their
importance, yet never confusing
my role with my Self.

57

SOURCE OF ALL BLESSINGS,

you bless us with falling stars,
as we look up into the glittering
vault of the sky on a mid-August
night and see the awesome cosmic
light show that has been going on
for eons before there were eyes to
watch it and will be going on when
no audience remains. When that
unpredictable flash happens, may I
make a wish that matters.

58

SOURCE OF ALL BLESSINGS,

you bless us with s u r f, with its
ever new moods and voices, its
thunder, its whisper, its hissing, its
growl, its groan, its laughter, its
music, its roar; with its shades of
gray and green and blue and brown
and its rainbows now and then;
with its spray, its foam, its spit;
and with its innumerable smells I
cannot name. May I, no matter how
far away from the ocean, hear, see,
smell, and feel it in my heart.

59

SOURCE OF ALL BLESSINGS,

you bless us with s h i p s —from
the walnut shells rigged with
oak leaf sails that we as children
floated on a pond to the cruise
ships of our retirement years;
from the yachts and freighters and
tankers passing on island horizons
to the tugboats pulling ocean liners
into port. May I still feel the thrill
of board planks under my feet,
still feel a sea breeze on my cheeks
when I set out on my last voyage.

60

SOURCE OF ALL BLESSINGS,

you bless us with hospitality —
most ancient of sacred human
agreements and one of the last
to remain sacred even in our so
secular world. Ever since I was
solemnly welcomed in the holy
precinct of a Maori moray on
Aotearoa, I know more deeply
what it means to be honored as
guest. May I extend a welcome to
all who, like me, are guests on this
earth, called to be hosts to one
another.

61

SOURCE OF ALL BLESSINGS,

you bless us with children's
toys—the dolls and teddy bears
that danced to our nursery rhymes,
the toy trucks and trains, wooden
swords, cardboard shields, and
paper helmets, the loved-to-death
rag doll, the fuzzy bunny rabbit
with his torn ear. It was real, that
love for our early companions. May
I never lose that love, but letting it
grow up, may I remember that all
things are toys we will sooner or
later outgrow.

62

SOURCE OF ALL BLESSINGS,

you bless us with y a w n i n g—that
good deep yawning, the body's
full confession to being (still or
already) sleepy, first the jaws
admitting it, then neck, shoulders,
back, and every muscle, down to
legs and toes. Relaxed and pajama-
drowsy, we smile sheepishly. May
I keep in readiness that smile, as
contagious as yawning itself, and
use its power to defuse tension.

63

SOURCE OF ALL BLESSINGS,

you bless us with elderberry
bushes—so sacred to our
forebears that as schoolboys we
were taught to doff our little hats
not only when we passed a church
but when we passed an elderberry
bush, heavy with ivory blossoms in
May and heavier still with purple
berries in September. We made
pipe stems from its hollowed-out
twigs, but we knew it was holy.
May I get an opportunity to pass
on to some children the lore of holy
trees.

64

SOURCE OF ALL BLESSINGS,

you bless us with generosity—
noblest of attitudes, so exalted
that it was associated with kings
and princes and received its name
from the well born, the gentility,
who could bestow bounty on their
retainers and benefits on those
whom normally they oppressed and
exploited. May I speak out loudly
for the dignity of the well-born
human heart, exalting its natural
generosity.

65

SOURCE OF ALL BLESSINGS,

you bless us with p a s s i n g
g l a n c e s —eyes that surprise our
eyes in a crowd, in a parking lot, or
a checkout line. Tired or sparkling,
harsh or mild, glinting furtively
and quickly turning away or calm
and gentle like the eyes of cows—
what lives touch my life in those
moments! May my own eyes be
alert to the gift of quick glances,
welcoming like ships hoisting
bright pennants in passing.

66

SOURCE OF ALL BLESSINGS,

you bless us with hats —
headdresses in all their variety:
hood, headband, top hat, fez,
helmet, dunce cap, yarmulke,
warbonnet, babushka, bridal
veil, shower cap, diadem, turban,
beanie, pillbox, crown, shesh,
tiara, and Irish Tam o' Shanter.
Some keep us from sunstroke, some
keep us warm, and some are of
little practical use, but all of them
make us feel a little taller. May I do
this to all I meet.

67

SOURCE OF ALL BLESSINGS,

you bless us with pilgrimage.
Be it to Mecca, Santiago, or
Jerusalem, it doesn't matter; not
even getting there matters much,
for every step is the goal, and what
might seem of no importance takes
on new significance: footgear,
weather, singing, sweat, tiredness,
silence, circumambulations. May
I not use the image of life as a
pilgrimage glibly. Every step is the
goal. May I act this out.

68

SOURCE OF ALL BLESSINGS,

you bless us with sleep, which
refreshes and renews our body
and gives our mind time to settle
like muddy water that turns clear.
Like a mother who comforts and
heals our restless hearts, deep
and dreamless sleep takes us
into her arms. May I be ready to
embrace sleep when sleep is ready
to embrace me, and let myself fall
with confidence into its fountain
of youth.

69

you bless us with flea markets
and garage sales—marvelous
opportunities for sellers to get rid
of cumbersome superfluity and
for buyers to discover unexpected
bargains; for those who step back
and watch the dynamics, this is
a quick and easy way to learn
a secret: The fun is not in the
possessing but in the buying and
selling. May I live by that secret
and celebrate exchange.

70

SOURCE OF ALL BLESSINGS,

you bless us with learning by heart—so altogether different from learning by rote; for when we learn by heart we do not memorize the sound of words but let the images evoked by words brand our hearts like red-hot branding irons. May I continue to encounter poets and sages worthy thus to shape my imagination, my worldview, my God view, my heart's landscape.

71

SOURCE OF ALL BLESSINGS,

you bless us with s o a p bubbles—
not two of them ever alike of the
thousands I have flown from my
nursery window, or year after year
as a birthday ritual, or on Easter
morning once, flocks of them
rising higher than the chapel's
steeple. May I taste fully the
delight I find in their shimmering,
soaring, spinning, and vanishing,
and pass it on by joyfully living in
the Now.

72

SOURCE OF ALL BLESSINGS,

you bless us with **thunderstorms**—
sudden ones that attack us on hikes
with a crash and a downpour that
drenches us to the bone, slow-
brewing ones that simmer all
of a stifling summer afternoon
until they boil over at nightfall,
green-lightning ones of June,
rock-shattering ones high in the
mountains, silent sheet lightning in
winter. May the awe they instill in
me keep me wide awake.

SOURCE OF ALL BLESSINGS,

you bless us with glass —its many
kinds and shapes and colors, the
glass of windowpanes, lightbulbs,
wine goblets, the nose cones of
missiles, the marbles and beach
glass that were our grade-school
treasures, the lenses of telescopes,
the beads that have spent centuries
in tombs, the tear bottles buried by
grieving women, glass that won't
ever decay yet shatters at once.
May it teach me to handle all things
with care.

74

you bless us with road crews.
Sometimes they slow us down, we
see faces and we wave, but mostly
they serve us unseen; in seconds
we zoom over stretches of road
that took weeks of hard labor to
build. May I be aware that mindful
driving includes mindfulness of all
the men and women who labor hard
to build our roads.

75

SOURCE OF ALL BLESSINGS,

you bless us with burial
grounds —the no-nonsense
cemeteries of the New World with
their close-cropped lawns and
markers level with the ground,
or Old World churchyards where
wrought-iron crosses watch over
beds of flowers in which the dead
sleep as under living quilts, or
pyramids, or prehistoric dolmen.
Reminders, all of them, welcome or
not; may I heed them.

76

SOURCE OF ALL BLESSINGS,

you bless us with palm trees—
the ones in their native sunshine,
rooted in the island sand of a
tropical beach or in a desert,
and the others, the exiles, potted
witnesses to a life in blessed
laziness, easygoing, laid-back, and
dreamy; yes, those most of all,
whose tattered fronds in fog and
icy drizzle still remind us of calm,
warm, moonlit nights. May I, too,
remember and witness to my true
home.

SOURCE OF ALL BLESSINGS,

you bless us with proverbs.
In my childhood, old sayings
were on everyone's tongue, as
comfortable as old shoes, and like
old shoes, in pairs, they often
came mirroring and contradicting
each other. Do "birds of a feather
flock together," or do "opposites
attract"? Is there maybe some truth
in both? May I learn from them to
look twice, to take everything with
a grain of salt, and to seek wisdom
in contradictions.

78

SOURCE OF ALL BLESSINGS,

you bless us with p o e m s —
most precious of all human
creations, "costing not less than
everything" in their simplicity,
most like creatures of God's own
creativity in the fragile unself-
conscious nakedness of Paradise.
They feed us with honey of the
mind; their music makes us soberly
drunk. May I feast on them every
day of my life and live each day as
a poem of praise.

79

SOURCE OF ALL BLESSINGS,

you bless us with summer
rain—starting with a smell all
its own when drizzle settles the
dust, turning into a calm flow, then
becoming a steady stream, sleepy
and unhurried, that falls all day
(and the next and the next, till time
stands still), making the earth soft
and rich and the grass green.
May I let its voice so quiet my
mind that I become for all around
me like mild rain.

80

SOURCE OF ALL BLESSINGS,

you bless us with c o w s —
most motherly toward us humans,
most nurturing. How many of
my ancestors may have survived
infancy because of a cow's milk?
How nourishing for our souls the
calm of cows, the leisure of their
chewing the cud, the patient glance
of their goddess eyes. May the
warmth of their flanks against my
cheek at milking time, the rich
smell of the barn, make me gentle
and kind.

81

SOURCE OF ALL BLESSINGS,

you bless us with a n g e l s —
those spirit messengers who come
in ever new and surprising forms.
To the ancients they were "the
Powers," overawing presences.
No image can do justice to their
mystery, but when we are alert,
we meet them everywhere. May I
sense them, heed them, and myself
become a messenger, for we are all
meant to be angels to one another.

82

SOURCE OF ALL BLESSINGS,

you bless us with church bells.
For centuries these bronze-tongued
messengers have called us together
to worship, awakened us in the
morning, reminded us at noon to
pray for peace, invited us, when
evening comes, to rest from work
and celebrate; they greet arriving
pilgrims and ring for our last
pilgrimage. May I hear them in my
heart, whether or not my ear does.

83

you bless us with b e d s , where we
are conceived, where we are born,
and where we die. What a blessing
to die in a bed, rather than in a
car crash or a bomb shelter. May
I never forget those who sleep in
the street; may I delight in even
a monastic cot, where it is warm
enough, where I can dream and
daydream and spin out some of my
most creative thoughts.

84

SOURCE OF ALL BLESSINGS,

you bless us with b i r d s o n g—
the ecstasy of a lark, still singing
as we lose sight of it in the blue
sky; the water music of the thrush
when the sun comes out after a
thunderstorm; the bell the cuckoo
keeps ringing on an island when
the hawthorn is in bloom. May I
remember my calling: to sing in
my heart with all the songbirds of
the world, for sheer gratitude and
to give joy to others by this silent
song.

85

SOURCE OF ALL BLESSINGS,

you bless us with b a s k e t s —
marvelously combining ancient
craftsmanship with ever new
skills; and usefulness in daily
life with artistic refinement.
How well their makers know and
utilize willows, reeds and rushes,
grasses, fibers, vines, and even the
baleen of whales for twisting and
weaving. May our communities
resemble baskets in their skill of
interweaving.

86

SOURCE OF ALL BLESSINGS,

you bless us with g a r d e n s —
flower gardens, dizzy from
fragrant abundance, or beds in
neat rows, but above all the garden
we dream of, with wall, well, and
white-gravel walkways, its bench
shaded by fruit trees, its arbor of
grapevines or roses, its fountain,
stone steps, statues, and box hedge.
May it flourish, that garden of my
imagination, anywhere, welcoming
in any weather.

87

SOURCE OF ALL BLESSINGS,

you bless us with soft eyes and voices—the far-off laughter of children across water, the glances of eyes filled with tears. They say so much, those voices sobered by silence; they see so much, those eyes mellowed by grief. May I welcome the world with gentle eyes that see so much more clearly than hard looks can; may I speak as tenderly to others as lovers do in summer twilight.

88

SOURCE OF ALL BLESSINGS,

you bless us with children's
questions —startling,
disconcerting, incessant; they
pop up like burps of wonderment
to challenge glib explanations,
wide-eyed toads surfacing from
undomesticated depths and as
determined to stay as the Frog
Prince. May I expose myself to
these helpful little time bombs,
whether offered by children I know
or by the child within, and may I
treasure their shock.

89

SOURCE OF ALL BLESSINGS,

you bless us with dragonflies—
their very name evoking happy
summer days, water and reeds, the
heat of high noon, deep-blue skies,
and a stillness so vast that I can
hear the glassy clinking of their
wings as they flit by. They have
been celebrating life like this for a
hundred million years. May I watch
with respect these old-timers,
learning from them as I stretch
lazily on the sun-warm deck.

90

SOURCE OF ALL BLESSINGS,

you bless us with teachers.
Without them, we would not
even be able to read the words
on this page, and yet, how little
appreciated they are in our society,
often shamefully treated, poorly
paid, seldom sufficiently thanked.
May I never forget the children
who have no schools, never forget
how much I owe my own teachers,
never forget to gratefully pray for
them.

91

SOURCE OF ALL BLESSINGS,

you bless us with r a i n b o w s —
little ones in dewdrops and
crystals, or huge ones from end to
end of the sky, it does not matter;
whenever they appear their magic
makes the heart leap with joy and
surprise. By their very nature we
can never reach them, never find
their end (or the pot of gold),
never walk through their arch.
May the thrill of intangible beauty
uphold me on dark days.

SOURCE OF ALL BLESSINGS,

you bless us with **unexcavated**
treasures—surprises dormant
for millennia in tombs, caves,
desert sands, and ocean depths,
or under highway embankments,
parking lots, or sidewalks.
Some will one day be as famous
as the Dead Sea Scrolls, the
Ardagh Chalice, or the Venus of
Willendorf. May I stay mindful
of the others that may never be
found and live close to impending
surprise.

93

SOURCE OF ALL BLESSINGS,

you bless us with b o o k s —
not only what's written in them but
the books themselves, the pages
between two covers, the spine,
the title page, the flyleaf, for the
feel of them in our hands, their
texture, weight, and smell. May
they continue to grace my life, the
paperback in my pocket and the
codex on the shelf no less than the
iPad that holds a whole library but
has no smell.

94

you bless us with resistance —
our freedom to take a stance,
to speak truth to power, to
defy, without counting the cost,
oppression, exploitation, and
aggression. May I never polarize
a situation by seeing things as
black and white, and may I never
yield to the temptation to oppose
violence violently, but may I find
the courage to stand up against the
domination system and witness to
God's reign of compassion.

95

SOURCE OF ALL BLESSINGS,

you bless us with fits and
misfits—colors that match and
colors that clash, harmony and
dissonance, soul mate and pain
in the neck. If nothing matched,
all would be chaos; if everything
fit, all would be stuck. When Aki
loves Bobbi who loves Cam who
in turn loves Aki, all three with
unrequited love, the play goes on,
and that's what life is all about.
May I stop looking for the perfect
fit and appreciate when things and
people do fit.

96

you bless us with **puppet shows**—
the essence of theater and mirror of
life, unabashed, outspoken make-
believe that grips and transforms.
Witch and princess, robber, king,
and dragon—all are played by
myself, all stripped from my hand
and put back in the box when
their part is finished. May I play
my many roles without getting
stuck in any of them, so that I can
thoroughly enjoy the playing.

97

SOURCE OF ALL BLESSINGS,

you bless us with s p i d e r s —
all the more of a gift for being so
difficult to appreciate. I admire
their intricate webs, yes, but only
when I conquer my initial disgust,
my spontaneous impulse to run
away, do I find the right attitude
and venture to take a closer look
at their hairy limbs that seem
always too many. May they teach
me to respect and honor even those
creatures with whom I will never
be friends.

98

SOURCE OF ALL BLESSINGS,

you bless us with migratory
birds—swallows that return each
spring to San Juan Capistrano as
promptly on schedule as the Swiss
railroad, robins that pop up on the
lawn one morning around Easter,
starlings that gather in clouds to
fly south before snowfall; and
the arctic terns I read about that
migrate from pole to pole. May
they remind me to be alert and
respond to my own life's times and
seasons.

99

SOURCE OF ALL BLESSINGS,

you bless us with unfinished
business—an unanswered letter,
that word I wanted to look up in
the dictionary all day, a phone
call that will have to wait till
tomorrow, and the bigger items on
my list, like the long-postponed
vacation, the book that wants to
be opened, the overdue apology.
May they make me sift out the
important from the urgent, tackle
it, and praise the perfection of the
unfinished.

100

SOURCE OF ALL BLESSINGS,

you bless us with . . .

May I . . .

INDEX

of blessings by number

index

index

A CLOSER LOOK AT
THE APOSTLES' CREED

In *Deeper Than Words*, Brother David Steindl-Rast reexamines the defining prayer of the early followers of Jesus, reading line-by-line with an open perspective to reveal the often overlooked message of faith, compassion, peace, love, and awareness that the Apostles' Creed represents.

Pages: 176 | ISBN: 978-0-307-58961-3| $12.00 US/ $14.00 CAN

ALSO AVAILABLE IN EBOOK FORMAT
Pages: 176 | ISBN: 978-0-307-58962-0| $9.99 US/ $9.99 CAN